CATHERINE CAWTHORNE   AYSHA

WE WENT TO FIND T. REX

Everybody ready? Only take what you **REALLY** need. Do we REALLY need your collection of special sticks? Yup!

TIME MACHINE

Fine. Let's head off to the time of the **dinosaurs!**

Shhhhh! Whatever-it-is might hear you!
Could it be a T. Rex?

T. Rexes were really big and heavy, weren't they?
Yes, but did they have... **beaks?**

That's not a T.Rex. It's a **Triceratops!**

Triceratops had an enormous skull, about a third of the length of its whole body. Imagine if humans had heads like that!

Nobody's certain what the big, thick, bony frill was for. It might have been to protect Triceratops's neck from predators, or to attract mates. Or it could have been a bit like wearing school uniform (but much cooler!) so that all the Triceratopses would recognise each other.

T.Rex was Triceratops's arch enemy. Triceratops fossils have been found with T.Rex bite marks on them! But Triceratops had those big pointy horns to defend itself. EPIC BATTLE!

This says we're in the Sahara Desert, but it doesn't look very **deserty!**

That's right – there were rivers and lakes all over here in dinosaur times.

Are we following a MASSIVE DUCK? Shhhhh, can anyone hear that noise?

That's not a T. Rex, it's a **Spinosaurus!**

Spinosaurus is the largest known predatory dinosaur. It was bigger than T. Rex or Giganotosaurus!

Spinosaurus was one of the few dinosaurs that ate lots of fish and spent time in the water. Unfortunately, dinosaurs didn't invent chips or ketchup to go with the fish. Can you imagine how boring their school dinners were? Poor Spinosauruses.

MENU
MONDAY - FISH
TUESDAY - MORE FISH
WEDNESDAY - JUST FISH
THURSDAY - PLAIN OLD FISH
FRIDAY - FISH 'N' FISH

Um, I think that massive sail might be a warning sign. Warning us to what? **SWIM FOR IT!**

Everything's sh–sh–sh–shaking again!
Were there earthquakes in
d–d–d–dinosaur t–t–times?
Or is it a WHOLE HERD of Triceratopses?

THUD **THUD** **THUD**

Ummmm . . . everyone . . .
don't . . . look . . . up!

That's not a T. Rex, that's a **Patagotitan!**

Patagotitan might be the largest dinosaur ever to have lived. It was ABSOLUTELY GINORMOUS! It weighed about as much as 12 African elephants and was longer than a blue whale.

It makes that Diplodocus over there look titchy!
Oh yeah! I thought Diplodocuses were massive,
but it's half as tall as Patagotitan!

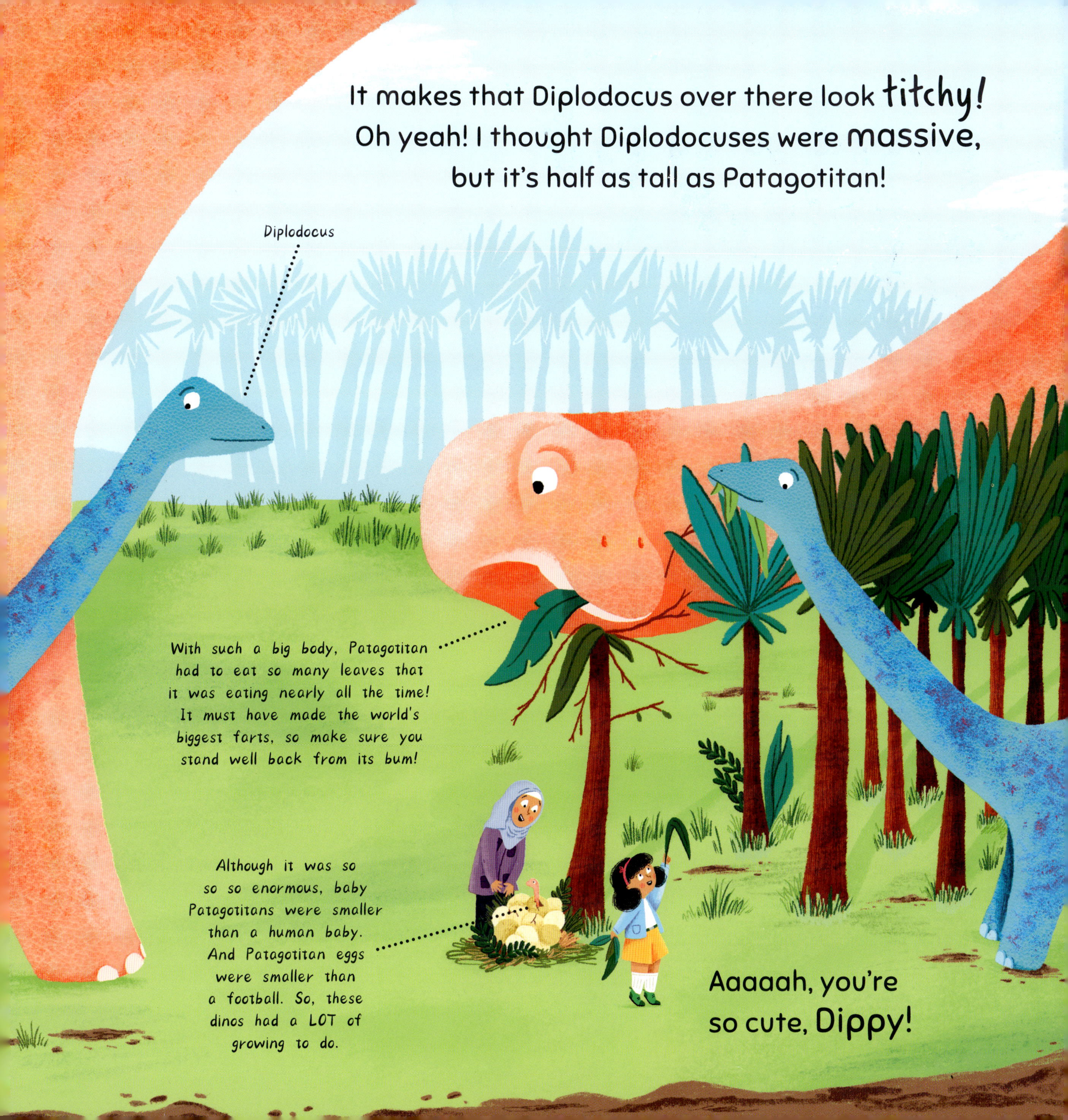

Diplodocus

With such a big body, Patagotitan had to eat so many leaves that it was eating nearly all the time! It must have made the world's biggest farts, so make sure you stand well back from its bum!

Although it was so so so enormous, baby Patagotitans were smaller than a human baby. And Patagotitan eggs were smaller than a football. So, these dinos had a LOT of growing to do.

Aaaaah, you're so cute, Dippy!

Coming, T.Rex, ready or not!
 Where aaaaaaare you?
Something is rustling over there.
Almost *definitely* a T.Rex.

Wait! These footprints have too many toes.

And what's with this strange, bumpy back? And this SPIKY, SWIPY TAIL?

That doesn't sound right...

That's not a T.Rex, it's a **Stegosaurus!**

Nobody's sure what the plates down the Stegosaurus's back were for. They could have given off heat to cool the body down, or soaked up heat from the Sun to warm up. Or the plates were how all the Stegosauruses recognised one another.

If you think that looks like a really teeny head on such a big dinosaur, you're right! The Stegosaurus had a very small head and brain for such a big body. So don't ask it to help you with your homework.

Do we need to get out of the way of that tail, before it wakes up?

It sounds like there are birds up there. Or T. Rexes.
T. Rexes didn't live in trees, did they?

Nope...
Well, there's something up there with feathers,
and it's not a pigeon!

T. Rex must be near, we've looked EVERYWHERE!
Wait, what's that?
Something really BIG...

With a HUGE JAW full of teeth...
And two stomping FEET...

We've found one! High five! It's a T. Rex!
Hang on a minute, why's it got HORNS on its head?

We thought that before!
And we don't want to be wrong... AGAIN.
Where's the T.Rex **Spotting** Checklist?

What a T.Rex looks like:
1. Massive jaws for crunching
2. Ridiculously short arms
3. ~~Breathes fire~~
4. Walks on two legs
5. ~~Cute fluffy ears~~
6. ENORMOUS!!!!

In its HUMONGOUS head, there were HUMONGOUS eyeballs! T. Rex had the largest eyes we know about of any land animal... ever. And it had really good vision for spotting you hiding or running away!

Watch out! T. Rex can **SEE** us easily, **CATCH** us easily and **EAT** us easily! Time to go home now?

Yep!

Everyone ... move .. away ...
from ... the ... T. Rex ...

Next time, shall we look for something less... dinosaurish?

Now that we're back, we can look for dinosaurs at home. But all the dinosaurs are extinct, silly! Well, actually, not all of them...

Birds belong to a group of dinosaurs called theropods. Theropods are the meat-eating dinosaurs that walked on two legs, like T.Rex, Carnotaurus, Spinosaurus and Microraptor.

So next time a pigeon poos on your head, you can tell everyone that a DINOSAUR pooed on your head!

Every single bird that's alive today is actually a dinosaur! Ducks quacking, chickens pecking, blackbirds chirping and seagulls nicking your chips are ALL dinosaurs!

Birds and lots of other theropod dinosaurs have hollow bones, which make them lighter. This helped dinosaurs to run faster. Just remember — don't EVER race a dinosaur.

Lots of dinosaurs also had feathers. But they weren't for flying. The feathers were probably for insulation (keeping warm) or display (showing off). Glamosaurus!

To Ethan, who understands the great importance of dinosaurs
C.C.

For Nabeelah
A.A.

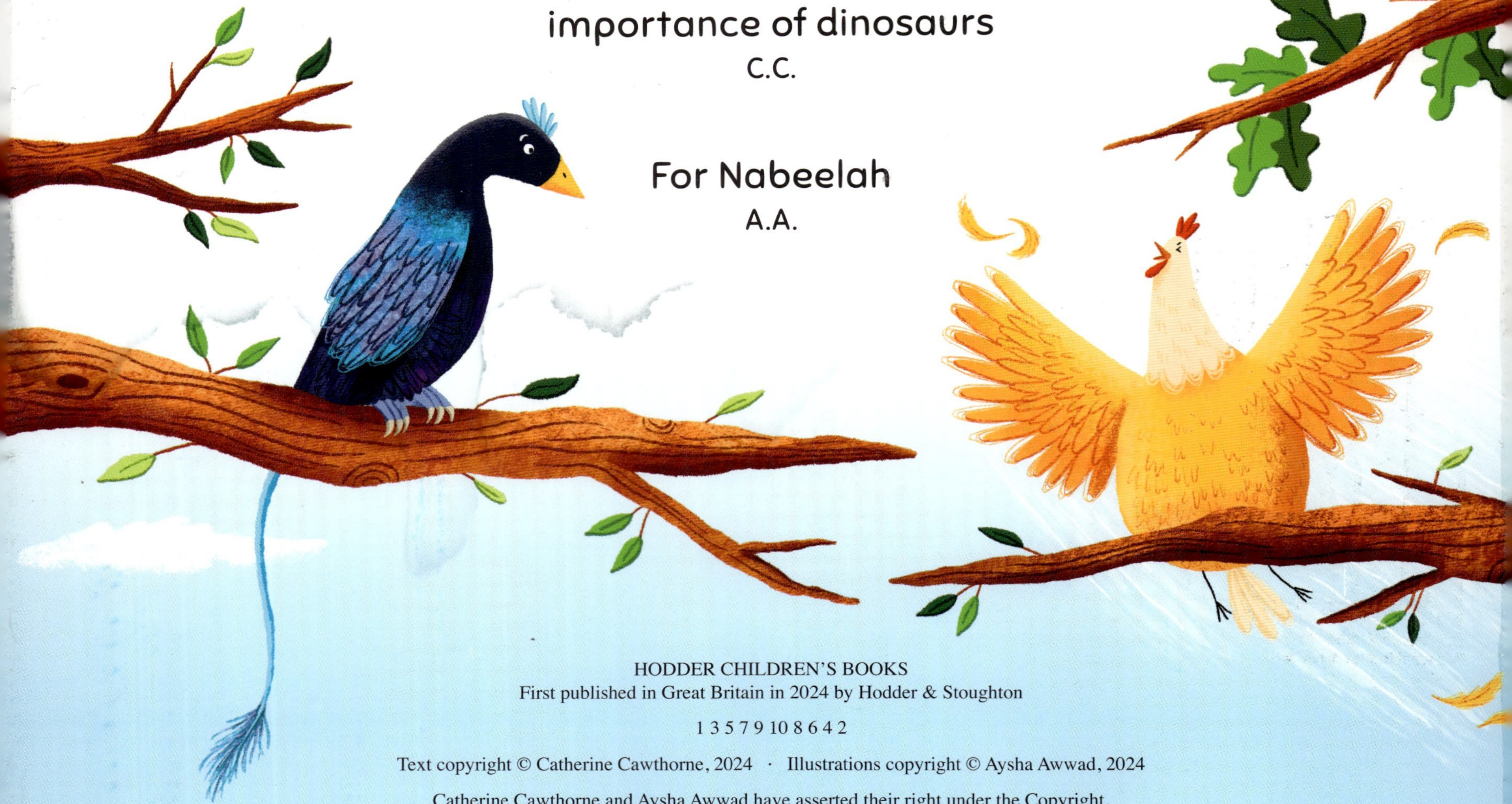

HODDER CHILDREN'S BOOKS
First published in Great Britain in 2024 by Hodder & Stoughton

1 3 5 7 9 10 8 6 4 2

Text copyright © Catherine Cawthorne, 2024 · Illustrations copyright © Aysha Awwad, 2024

Catherine Cawthorne and Aysha Awwad have asserted their right under the Copyright,
Designs and Patents Act 1988, to be identified as the author and illustrator of this work.
All rights reserved. A CIP catalogue record for this book is available from the British Library.

PB ISBN 987-1-526-36561-3 · E-book ISBN 978-1-444-97363-1
Printed in China

Hodder Children's Books
An imprint of Hachette Children's Group
Part of Hodder & Stoughton Limited
Carmelite House, 50 Victoria Embankment, London, EC4Y 0DZ

An Hachette UK Company
www.hachette.co.uk

www.hachettechildrens.co.uk